BIGFOOT FIELD GUIDE MAGAZINE

Contents

Bigfoot Field Guide Magazine is published by Mid-America Bigfoot Research Center, the largest active Bigfoot Research organization in North America.

To contact the *Bigfoot Field Guide Magazine* staff, please e-mail:

darkwinglh@gmail.com

FROM THE EDITOR'S DESK

The irony of woo.

I've been involved now with the Bigfoot Community since 1991, when I began in earnest to investigate sightings of Bigfoot. It would take nearly a decade for my first encounter to occur and it would drastically change my life.

The Bigfoot Community then was rather small, everyone knew everyone else, and the research was steeped in common-sense. There was no woo to it. The community as a whole, believed steadfastly that Bigfoot was a flesh and blood animal that did not have any paranormal abilities. It hid very well, and stayed away from humans and civilization.

The woo factor started seeping into the community with the advent of Facebook, where erroneous information could be passed nearly at the speed of light, once it was posted, there were many who believed anything as long as it was on the Internet. It's on the Internet, it must be true!! Unfortunately, there is more disinformation out there than there is legitimate information about Bigfoot. It seems anyone can post what they think, and there are people gullible enough to believe what is being claimed.

A child psychologist in Oregon makes claims that Bigfoot can cloak, opens portals and travels between dimensions, and literally thousands of people who follow his hilarious antics, buy into what he claims, despite his ability to provide any evidence to back up his claims.

Another individual in Oklahoma claims she is descended from Cherokee/Creek medicine people, using this as a lead in for her claims of being one with Bigfoot. Yet gets busted by the Feds for selling items she claims are Native American made, but can't provide any proof of her so called Native American heritage.

And third, an author claims that Bigfoot travels to him in his thoughts and dreams, becoming a teacher to him.

The woo is strong in these folks, and yet, we have those gullible enough to believe every word they say, some to the extent of threatening others with retaliation for even daring to criticize these folks.

My best advice to anyone entering into the Bigfoot Community these days, as the great Ray Crowe said, "Wear your skeptical!!" Always be skeptical of everything you are told, use your common sense to see through the bullsh*t!!

The Editor

IN MEMORIAM

Wayne Mormann

MABRC Organizational Member and Research Wayne Mormann left this world on December 6th, 2015. This issue of the Bigfoot Field Guide Magazine is dedicated to him.

We hope that he finds a great place to sit beside a stream up in Heaven, and drink cold ones all day, maybe with a Bigfoot sitting there drinking with him.

Oklahoma Bigfoot Symposium

T-Shirts

Oklahoma Bigfoot Symposium t-shirts are still available for purchase, these incredible shirts come in either black or grey colors, in various sizes.

Prices:

$15.00 for small - XL and $18.00 for 2&3 XL. Plus shipping

To order, email at
gma.pa1@outlook.com

MABRC Researcher Spotlight

Name: Rick Stancombe
Location: Bloomington, Indiana
Occupation: Being a great dad
Marital Status: Married (25 to life)
Kids: 1 son; Maxwell Robert
Hobbies: Son, Playing on the computer, Squatching research
Favorite activity: sleeping
Favorite Food: Pizza
Favorite movie/TV Show: Poseidon Adventure, Aliens, Kelly's Heroes, T.V. ; Falling Skies, Terra Nova, Primeval, Dr.Who, Destination Truth.
How did you get started into squatching? Heard about him all my life, scared of it as a kid, Boggy Creek made me even more scared. took a major interest in it after the Georgia hoax. Read lots of info on Stinky and a lot of History. Which makes my belief in this creature stronger.

Funniest Squatching Story: None of my own. Cant remember who it was on this site. But they told of a boy going to an Outhouse at night, he tried to open the door and the door slammed shut, he pulled on it again and there was a big hairy guy standing there, the Boy went screaming back into the house. I know it wasnt funny for him, but it has always made me chuckle. I try to imagine the look on both of there faces.

What would you do if confronted with an angry Squatch? Quick prayer, and do a docile ape movement, and avoid eye contact.
Best advice to anyone who wants to go Squatching? **LEAVE YOUR CAMERA ON! ALWAYS!**
If you could go back and relive a moment, what would it be and would you change anything? My whole life! Except for my wife and son.

Rick "Mono Grande" Stancombe

Senior Field Researcher

Video Analysis Guide

Learn how to do your own Video Analysis

Own your very own copy of the Bigfoot Field Guide—In the Shadows, Video Analysis in Bigfoot Research. Learn how to do your own video analysis just like the researchers of the **MABRC** do it. Step by step guides on how to install the software needed, to how to use it. It's all here in an easy to use format.

Available now on Amazon, at http://www.amazon.com/Shadows-Video-Analysis-Bigfoot-Research-ebook/dp/B00S3F58EM

Or at Createspace at https://www.createspace.com/5021191

Featured Research Group

By J. Robert Swain

Arkansas has a rich, deep history in the search for Bigfoot. One of the first, if not the very first, nation-wide Bigfoot encounter was reported in newspapers as far back as 1834. Most of us researchers today cut our teeth on the campy 1971 movie, Legend of Boggy Creek situated in Fouke, Arkansas. In spite of key Bigfoot milestones like these mentioned, research in Arkansas has been left relatively isolated. The MABRC is headquartered in Oklahoma, the North American Wood Ape Conservancy is headquartered in Texas, TexLa is in Louisiana and Texas, the BFRO is mainly on the west coast and the GCBRO is deeper south. All of these groups and probably others have shown interest in Arkansas but there have been very few home-grown groups to cover the natural state. Although there are some small regional groups in northern and northwestern Arkansas, no group saw the entire state of Arkansas as their primary research area until the creation of Arkansas Primate Evidence Society.

Arkansas Primate Evidence Society, or APES as we call ourselves, loosely began in 2007 with me, Robert Swain, and my son Jamie, when we began to camp in areas well-known to be active. With wood knock and rock clack activity of our own in the wildlife management areas below Helena and west of Ashdown, we decided to invite some of our long-time friends to join us in the hunt. Frankie Parks and Taylor Francis were the first members. For several years we kept APES a locally closed group of just friends from church and work. With the advent of Facebook pages we were able to post our findings and invite others to the APES page. The group has slowly grown to about 30 members from several states.

Jason Kauntze inspecting footprints

APES strives to be a casual group of friends who research together. We have no dues and are family friendly. On our expeditions, visitors are welcome as long as they are willing to sign a liability release form. Everyone attending is responsible for his/her own camping and research equipment, meals and snacks. APES does not charge for their expeditions and if members or visitors find any evidence on an APES expeditions, it belongs to the finder. We only ask that the information and evidence be shared with the APES groups for its records.

APES has researched all over the state of Arkansas but since most of our members live in the central part of the state, most of our research is conducted in the central portion of Arkansas. We have two main research areas that have delivered footprints, dozens of impressive audio samples and one confirmed sighting by an APES member.

In 2015, after a couple of false starts due to tornados and bad weather, the APES group hosted the first Arkansas Bigfoot Conference in Vilonia, Arkansas. Some 250 people attended and there were three regional Bigfoot research groups represented. Also in 2015, APES hosted the Bigfoot Bootcamp, a family friendly campout with presentations about how to make a cast, types of research equipment and a walkthrough obstacle course of tree breaks and other possible Bigfoot structures to look for in the woods. The 2016 Arkansas Bigfoot Conference is scheduled for Saturday, April 23rd, 2016. Members of the MABRC will once again be in the speaker lineup for 2016.

One of our main goals as a research group is to educate the public about the possibility of Bigfoot being in Arkansas, not just in the Pacific Northwest. Members of APES conduct school presentations each year about the evidence of Bigfoot, what to look for and safety in the woods.

Other goals that we have as a group is to keep confidentiality when it comes to witnesses and reports. We also attempt to co-operate with other researchers and groups as much as possible. We have a longtime relationship with the MABRC, with some of our members being in both groups. APES and the MABRC have participated in joint expeditions and research projects like the Silent Hill Project.

APES is also compiling a sightings Bigfoot database of all known Arkansas reports. At the present time we have about 900 Bigfoot encounters in the database from 1800's to the present. All seventy-five counties in Arkansas have reported Bigfoot activity. We would very much like to know of any sightings or encounters that any reader may know of which have taken place in Arkansas.

If you know of a sighting to add to our database or would like to know more about APES… Please contact us at Robert@ArkansasApes.org

D.W. Lee, Executive Director, MABRC, Robert Swain, Director, APES, Alton Higgins, Chairman, NAWAC, at Arkansas Bigfoot Conference 2015

Robert Swain serves as the director of the Arkansas Primate Evidence Society. He is a long-time friend of the MABRC and a regular presenter at the Oklahoma Symposium. He serves on the board of the Alliance of Independent Bigfoot Researchers. He is also the artist and author of Laughsquatch: Book One and the illustrator for the children's book Patty: A Sasquatch Story. In the real world, Robert serves as a minister for the church of Christ. He and his wife and son live in Vilonia, Arkansas.

Make your plans now to attend!!!

2016 ARKANSAS BIGFOOT CONFERENCE

Saturday, April 23, 2016
8am to 5pm

Vilonia, Arkansas Municipal Building

sponsored by

Arkansas Primate Evidence Society

Robert@ArkansasApes.com

Bluff Creek Project

Logo of the Bluff Creek Project, art by Wes Losner

One of the better Bigfoot-related research projects going today is the **Bluff Creek Project**, originally started to locate and identify the original location of the Patterson-Gimlin Footage from 1967. Starting from it's grass roots even earlier by individuals, it

started coming together into an actual project in 2009, with the original members banding togeth-

er.

After subjecting a massive amount of time and money into the project, the location of the PGF was finally made official in the summer of 2011. Detailed surveys located many of the trees that were present in the original film, and put down on a map to aid in giving more exact dimensional data for the review of the original film.

The second phase of the project was initiated, in which trail cams would be placed in the immediate vicinity, not just to try and capture photos of any Bigfoot in the area, but also various other wildlife that was in the area. This phase though forced the team to ask for donations in order to purchase more

trail cams and of course, the batteries that were needed to keep them in continuous operation.

The most important achievement to date of the trail cam project, in my opinion, is the photos taken of the Humboldt Marten, a cousin of the weasel that is currently considered nearly extinct.

One of the original game cam photos from Bluff Creek above, the project has many other pictures of this small mammal moving back and forth along the water.

Another great achievement was the photos of a small bear in nearly the same position as the animal in the Jacob's photo taken in Pennsylvania, several years ago, and promoted by many to be a juvenile Bigfoot. Discussions with Dr. Jeff Meldrum in the past has shown that Dr. Meldrum and other scientists have considered the Jacob's

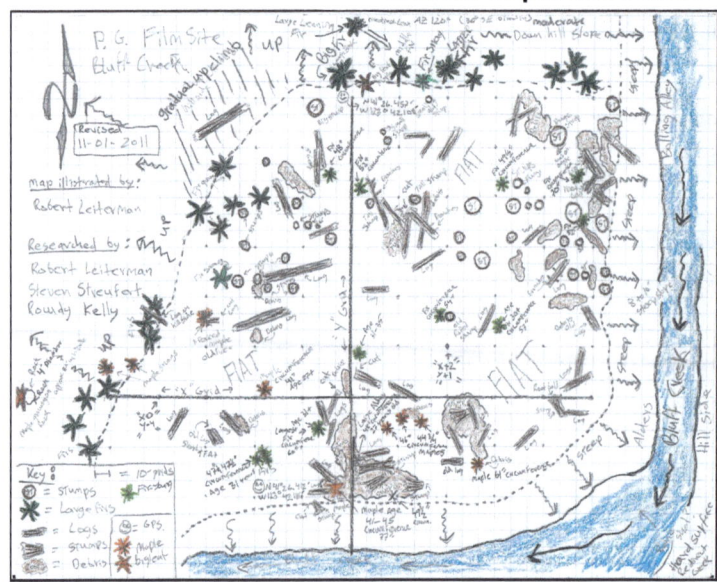

Creature to be nothing more than just a bear, despite some who cling to the hopes it's a juvenile Bigfoot, I think the photo taken by the **Bluff Creek Project** to be pretty convincing that it's nothing more than just a bear.

As you can tell, the legs of the bear in the **Bluff Creek Project** photo match up nearly perfectly with the same legs in the **Jacob's Creature** photo. The presence of other bear cubs in the Jacob's photos, before and after, makes it far-fetched to believe a juvenile Bigfoot would be in close proximity to them, given the motherly instincts exhibited by mother bears towards their young.

So we have three successes for the **Bluff Creek Project**, identifying the PGF site, photos of the Humboldt Marten, and now corroborating evidence that the Jacob's Creature is nothing more than a young bear bent over.

Now what does the **Bluff Creek Project** have on their agenda, they plan on continuing the trail camera project as long as funding continues, I would like to recommend that anyone who can donate to the project, please do so. The wildlife being photographed in this project is also critical for wildlife conservation efforts, and should always be of the utmost concern for all Bigfoot Researchers. To learn more about donating time or money to the project, visit their websites listed at the end of this article.

And now, for something that I do commend personally to the members of the **Bluff Creek** project. (Although the following isn't an actual Project objective, some of it's members were involved in it, so it's posted here with the project) For years, Matthew Johnson has been making some very absurd claims about a research location that he refers to as **SOHA** (Southern Oregon Habituation Area) in which he has claimed the **Bigfoot** there cloak, open portals, speak

The Bluff Creek Project photo above.

The Jacob's Creature Photo above.

to him, and even chose him to be a teacher to the younger Bigfoot there. What has been very frustrating to the real Bigfoot researchers is that people seem to follow Matthew Johnson's research like a religious cult.

Matthew would only take certain hand-picked individuals to **SOHA**, after they signed nondisclosure agreements, to see what was there. Conflicting accounts only further muddied the waters about what was going on there.

Most credible **Bigfoot** researchers have blown off Johnson's claims, as he provides no evidence to back up his claims, simply telling everyone that they have to believe him, because he says it's that way.

Steven Streufert and Jamie Wayne of the Bluff Creek Project, with the aid of a vast network of participants, finally located where **SOHA** was at.

At the end of 2015, the duo made a trip to the location to confirm if it had been located for sure.

The following comparison photos were taken against those posted by Matthew Johnson, and it was confirmed as the right location.

Future plans are for the Bluff Creek Project to go back to the location, in hopes of either replicating Matthew's claims, or to disprove his claims. Either way, while the **MABRC** and myself look down on invading another researcher's area, we do  (cont. on next page)

Matthew Johnson's photo of SOHA of his campsite.

Jamie's truck at the same location.

A different view of Johnson's camp at SOHA.

A view of the camp at SOHA with Jamie in the pic.

stand behind the **Bluff Creek Project** on this, as when someone makes outlandish and wild claims about an area, but refuse to present evidence to back up their claim or allow peer review of the area without being forced to sign an **NDA**, then it's necessary for the Bigfoot community to police itself.

The **MABRC** has allowed many individuals and groups into their research areas to ascertain the level of activity without **NDAs**, just the promise to keep the locations secret. If Matthew would have done the same thing, and accepted the findings of others without the threats that he has done in the past, the **Bluff Creek Project** would not have had to do this.

I personally can't wait to see what this team of folks can come up with in the future, I would like to thank them for what they have accomplished and wish them nothing but good luck in their future endeavors.

Bluff Creek Trail Camera Project, 2012-present, is: Jamie Wayne Rowdy Kelley Robert Leiterman Steven Streufert Kipp Morrill with Michael Meraz.

2012, with Munns, Louse Camp on Bluff Creek

Jamie Wayne is the one who administers the Trail Camera Project, for the most part.

2012 PGF site confirmation group

Bluff Creek Project Blog:

http://bluffcreekproject.blogspot.com/

Bigfoot Books Blog for additional information:

http://bigfootbooksblog.blogspot.com/

With USFS reps, PGF site

As noted previously, the links to the Bluff Creek Project's website and to Steven Streufert's blog are listed here, check them out for further information about the project, and I would like to thank Steven for all the information and photos supplied for this article. Without his help, I wouldn't have been able to write this.

Reporting a Sighting

The importance of turning in a sighting report is critical to Bigfoot Research, details from a sighting can be incorporated into a large database to formulate information that can show patterns in Bigfoot behavior, increasing the overall knowledge about the creatures.

If you have a sighting, there are numerous organizations out there to report it to, and at the MABRC, we take sighting reports through our website at http://www.mid-americabigfoot.com

Please give us contact information so that a researcher can contact you with further questions if necessary. All contact and location information is kept confidential to insure the witness' privacy.

Remember, Bigfoot Research can only grow through information.

Project Silent Hills

In **Bigfoot** research, researchers have long heard vocalizations and other noises associated as being created by Bigfoot. Most researchers have become accustomed to these vocalizations and noises, believing that they were occurring at great distances away from them. To ascertain the actual distance that researchers are hearing these different noises, the **MABRC** and **APES** groups conducted an experiment. The experiment was to determine at what distance these noises were viable to be heard by the human ear, with ambient noise, location and distance factored in.

What was discovered was eye opening to the researchers involved.

Special Recognition goes to Randy "Rebelistic" Savig and Bernie "Old hippy" Wall who originally discovered the background information needed to put this project/experiment into an active route. Their ground breaking work is very much appreciated.

Participants:

From the Mid-America Bigfoot Research Center

D.W. "Darkwing" Lee

Izzy "Goose" Gutierrez

Mike "CompresserMike" Hartsell

Dave "Squatchfinder" Ganote

Randy "Rebelistic" Savig

Mark "Sawdustt" Newbill (Also an APES member)

From the Arkansas Primates Evidence Society

Robert "Laughsquatch" Swain

The Experiment:

A set pattern of sounds was decided upon, this insured that the participants knew in which order they would be done, easier for documentation purposes.

The order is as given.

- Oak tree wood knock.
- Cedar tree wood knock.
- Red percussion block
- Green percussion block
- Human vocalization
- Call blaster

In all instances, the listening team would listen from the road, which was line-of-sight to the team creating the sounds, and then step into the woods in order to see if the audio became distorted from the vegetation.

The following is the data pertaining to three distinct distances between the sound team, and the listening team. For the sake of not having to move the sound generating hardware, the listening team moved away from the sound team.

The distances are listed with the data pertaining to each point the listening team stopped at. The distance was confirmed with a laser range finder.

Decibel Meters, used to detect the given range of noises were used to measure the range of the target noises used in the experiment.

Equipment used:

To conduct the experiment, certain equipment would be needed.

For the wood knocks on trees, a hickory axe handle was acquired.

What was noticed is that it's not the different types of trees that make the different tones of the wood knocks, it's the type of knocker used against the tree. An oak tree sounds just the same as a cedar, pine or even a hickory tree.

Here is the wood knocker used for this experiment.

Measurement devices:

To measure the Dba (or decibels) of the sounds being created, 2 decibel meters were purchased,

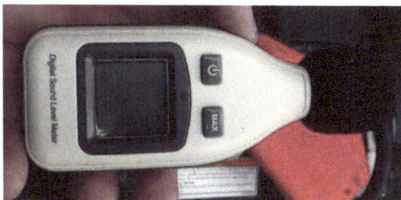

each one capable of doing a max decibel reading, in which, the loudest noises would show as the max reading. This allowed the research team to monitor the individual noises to see if they breached the ambient sound.

A laser rangefinder was also bought in order to get the actual distance from the sound team to the listening team. This one could register up to 800 yards.

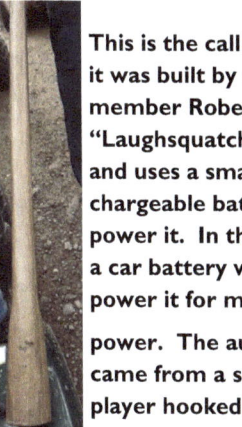

This is the call blast unit, it was built by **APES** member Robert "Laughsquatch" Swain, and uses a small rechargeable battery to power it. In this instance, a car battery was used to power it for maximum power. The audio files came from a small MP3 player hooked to the system.

Two different percussion blocks were used, both are pictured here.

The drumstick used, the thicker back end was used to strike the percussion blocks.

Sound level example chart:

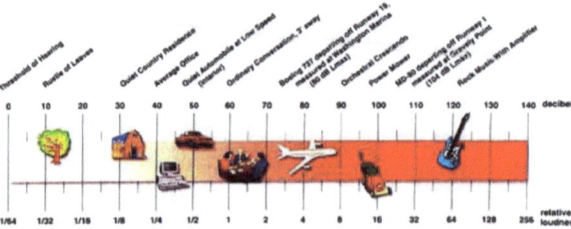

TYPICAL SOUND LEVELS

The **decibel (dB)** is a unit for describing sound pressure levels. A-weighted sound measurements (dBA) are filtered to reduce the effect of very low and very high frequencies, better representing human hearing. With A-weighting, sound monitoring equipment approximates the human ear's sensitivities to the different sounds of frequencies.

Baseline of sounds used:

After locating the area that the experiment would be held at, the team needed to obtain the baseline readings for each sound. Holding the Decibel meter at average of 3 feet from each sound being created, 3 times each sound was measured to obtain the base (average) reading of the sound level that was used. The levels are listed below with their average decibel level. The call blast unit was not measured for an average as it was going to be the same level due to the sound settings.

- Using wood handle made of Hickory:

Cedar Tree: 92.5, 93.7, 94.1 Average 93.4 Dba

Oak Tree: 97, 96.4, 95.8 Average 96.4 Dba

- Using snare drumstick, the thicker end.

Red percussion block: 110.8, 110.1, 120.6 Average 113.8 Dba

Green percussion block: 117.3, 118.1, 118.6 Average 118 Dba

- Using the call blast unit, we measured according to the volume control on the unit.

Call Blast unit – Ohio Howl

Setting 5: 114.7 Dba

Setting 10: 122.4 Dba

Setting 15: 127.8 Dba

Setting 20: 130.9 Dba

- Mike "Compressermike" Hartsell and Randy "Rebelistic" Savig both did vocalizations, an average was done for both.

Mike's Whoop: 113.6, 109.9, 112.3 Average 111.9 Dba

Randy's Whoop: 107.5, 108.4, 107.1 Average 107.7 Dba

<u>135 yards = 405 feet</u>

- Ambient noise 46.6 Dba
- Cedar No register
- Oak No register
- Red Percussion block 75 72.7 74.1 Dba
- Green Percussion block 72.3 69.2 Dba third done in trees nothing registers
- Call blast 79.7 78.8 Dba
- Whoop 65.1 69.0 Dba

<u>219 yards = 657 feet</u>

- Ambient noise level 46.5 Dba
- Cedar No register
- Oak No register
- Ambient Noise level 69.1 Dba
- Red Percussion block 72.6 Dba
- From woods 58.5 Dba

- Ambient noise level 62.8 Dba

- Green Percussion block 68.2 Dba

- Call blast 67.7 Dba

    From woods 60.2 Dba

- Ambient Noise level 59.8 Dba

    Whoop 63.4 Dba

    Woods No register

311 yards = 933 feet

- Ambient noise level 50.1 Dba

    Cedar Wood Knock
        None

- Ambient noise level 45.5 Dba

    Oak Wood Knock None

    Ambient Noise 65.7   Dba

    Red percussion block   67.3 Dba

From woods 61 Dba ambient noise

- Ambient Noise level 63 Dba

    Green percussion block 66.3 Dba

From woods 53.4 Dba ambient noise

- Call Blast 66.4 Dba

- Call Blast from woods 64.1

- Ambient noise level 59.3 Dba

Whoop 61.3 Dba

From woods ambient noise level 53.2 Dba

Tree Knock doesn't carry as far:

Conclusion

The data clearly shows that the wood knocks occur closer than most researchers have originally believed. If you hear a loud wood knock, it's within 200 feet or less from you. If you can hear the wood knock at all, its within 1,000 feet of your position.

The use of the percussion blocks have produced sounds that have

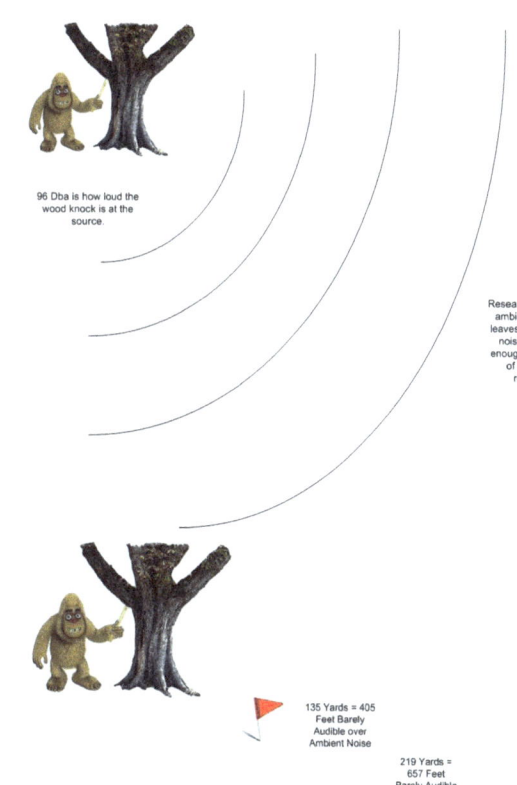

96 Dba is how loud the wood knock is at the source.

Researcher is 1000 feet away, with ambient noise (noise from wind, leaves and insects) of 50 Dba, the noise of the wood knock is not enough to overcome the loudness of the ambient sound. The researcher can't hear it.

135 Yards = 405 Feet Barely Audible over Ambient Noise

219 Yards = 657 Feet Baraly Audible over Ambient Noise, only because listening team was listening for it.

311 Yards = 933 Feet Only heard the wood knock because the listening team was expecting it.

been heard at greater distances, but from comments made from the base camp, nearly a mile away from the test site, the knocks caused by the blocks sounded like plastic being used to produce the knocks.

The vocalization used by the call blaster was the Ohio Howl, and was clearly heard up to a mile away by the base camp, this shows that the vocalization does carry further, and further research needs to be done on this part of the experiment.

Future plans for project

- Reprise the experiment during the winter months to cut down on ambient noise.

- Locate an area with longer distances to conduct further research. Replicate the experiment.

- Using rock clacks in future experiments.

- Reprise the experiment with different terrain types.

- Using parabolics and recorders in future experiments.

- Using thermal cameras to record the surrounding areas during the experiments in case the noises bring in Bigfoot close to the experiment area.

Arkansas Primate Evidence Society APES

MABRC Evidence Review Board

The **MABRC** has taken a bold step into the right direction with the creation of the Evidence Review Board, in order to have evidence submitted to the **MABRC** by it's researchers and by independent researchers.

The Board is composed of **7 MABRC** Organizational members who have backgrounds in various disciplines in Bigfoot research, and at times will call upon other members with their expertise to aid them in examining evidence.

The main reason behind the creation of the board, is that evidence presented by **MABRC** Researchers who wish to have the **MABRC** stand behind their evidence, has to pass muster through the Board before the organization will

This is not Proof – it is evidence!

attach the **MABRC** name to the evidence.

Even then, it will be attached as "possible" or "probable" Bigfoot evidence.

The **MABRC** feels as a whole, that most evidence can only be classified in this manner, until

a voucher specimen is obtained to confirm evidence that is held in the possession of many researchers.

The types of evidence range from audio, video, photographic to even physical, including casts, blood samples and hair samples, among other items.

Upon evaluation of the evidence, it requires a majority vote of the

Board to qualify it with the **MABRC** standing behind it as "possible" or "probable" evidence.

The members of the board are:

3GResearch

Rebelistic

TherealsuperDave

Holotype

Sawdustt

CompresserMike

Frogman

To submit evidence to the review board, contact the review board at the **MABRC** Website.

www.mid-americabigfoot.com

And click on the Evidence Review Board tab.

Equipment Corner

Catalytic Heaters

One part of Bigfoot research deals with being out during the winter hours, whether conducting expeditions, camping out or just sitting huddled somewhere listening for activity.

Part of my winter gear includes a catalytic heater complete with several small propane bottles in which I can heat my tent, my car or just prop it up near me while hunkered down by a rock or tree.

There are many variants, as shown in the following photos.

The portable type I use, hard to knock over due to the tilt it employs with it's legs.

And then there is the Mr. Buddy style heater that uses portable propane tanks, or with the adapter, you can hook it up to larger 5 gallon propane tanks for longer heating duration. Many MABRC researchers use these type of heaters in their tents to keep them warm at night.

It's recommended though, that when using these types of heaters under any conditions, they you should always maintain plenty of venting for the fumes and allow fresh air to enter a confined space. Also, take care to keep combustibles away from the heating elements. While these heaters do not use an open flame, they do get hot.

Oklahoma Bigfoot Symposium 2015

The 2015 Oklahoma Bigfoot Symposium was an outstanding success, as the **MABRC** invited speakers from **APES, TBRG,** and **BFRO.** Attendance was increased over the period of two days, with speakers on the first day, with a Town Hall meeting on the second day.

Door prizes were handed out, along with Bigfoot whistles to all the kids who were present.

Speakers were Ron Boles-**BFRO,** David Holley-**TBRG,** Robert Swain-**APES,** Randy Savig-**MABRC,** Jim White-

head-**MABRC,** and D.W. Lee-**MABRC.**

This is the 4th year of the Symposium, and next year, the planning is hoping to be for the best one yet.

Henri Edge also was promoted to Senior Field Researcher at the event, for her hard work and eagerness to learn everything she can.

There was even an appearance by Bigfoot himself, as he min

gled with the audience members and thrilled the youngsters with his growling and playing around with them.

Make sure to attend next year's symposium on the first weekend of October in Stilwell, Oklahoma and even come out and camp with the **MABRC** researchers in one of the best prime locations for Bigfoot activity in the state of Oklahoma.

Giving Bigfoot a hand

The illustrated casts of a hand print and a knuckle print were made from impressions found by Paul Freeman in the Blue Mountains, Washington.

The hand print was found in 1995, and the knuckle print in 1982. A footprint, 16 inches long, was found near the hand print. The human hand shown is that of a large man, about 6 feet tall and weighing about 215 pounds. (It needs to be noted that the knuckle illustration should be that of a left human hand rather than right.)

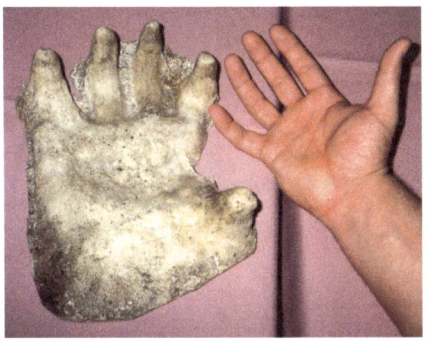

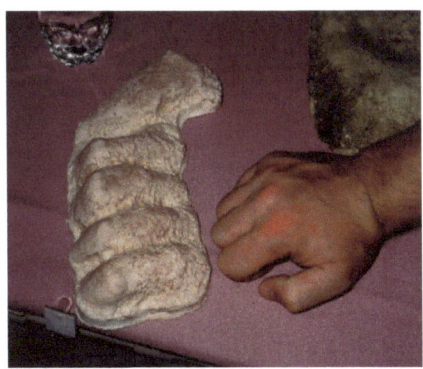

In February 1962, a sasquatch purportedly to have left a muddy hand print on the side of a white house in Fort Bragg, California. The creature had tried to enter the house. The 11.5-inch print was traced and compared to a man's hand.

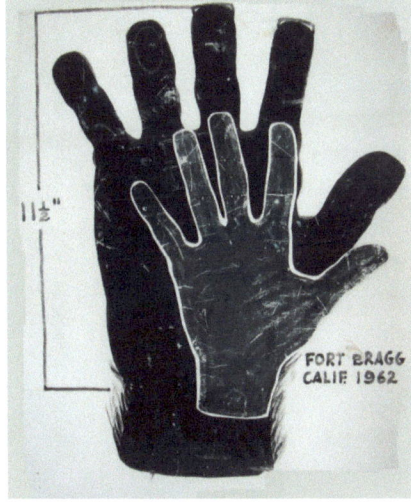

A more detailed scale drawing of the Fort Bragg hand print compared to a man's hand (man about 6 feet tall,190 pounds). The origination of the drawing is not known. It was sent to John Green and surfaced in about 2002.

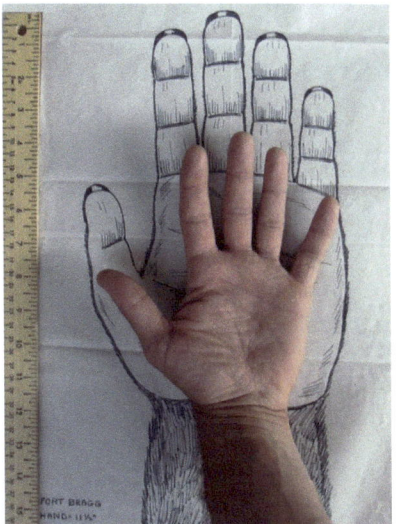

A scaled comparison between the cast of a human hand and the alleged sasquatch hand cast. The human cast has been photographically enlarged to match the size (height) of the sasquatch cast. The difference in the appearance of the casts is highly obvious.

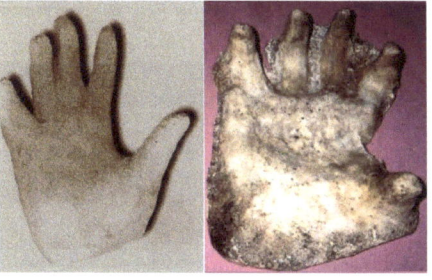

Concerning the hand print, Dr. Henner Fahrenbach states that the accompanying footprint indicates a creature about 7 feet, 4 inches (2.2 m) in height. His analysis of the hand print is as follows: The fingers may appear shorter and more pointed than they are in reality since sand had started to drift down into the holes left by the fingers. The print is remarkable for the absence of the thenar pad (the bulge at the base of the thumb) and the visibility of the finger tendons within the palm if the cast is held at an angle to a sharp light, both factors indicating a low level of opposability of the thumb. Its width at the palm is also fairly low in comparison to the largest, though less complete, prints that have been found.

A hand print found in mud at the bottom of a shallow pool on Onion Mountain, California, by Bob Titmus in 1982. Titmus drained the pool to get a cast of the print.

A human hand is shown to illustrate how the print was positioned.

just below the embankment where the hand print was located at.

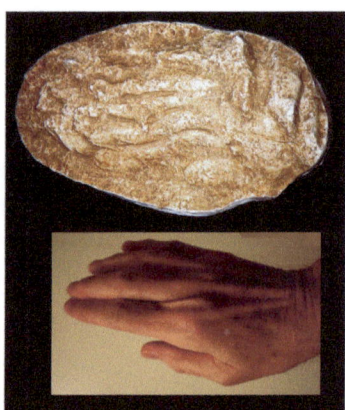

The **MABRC** has also cast a hand print and knuckle prints in Oklahoma. It took some ingenuity on the part of the researchers who cast the handprint, since it was on the side of an embankment. Their resourcefulness has provided us with another key piece of the puzzle.

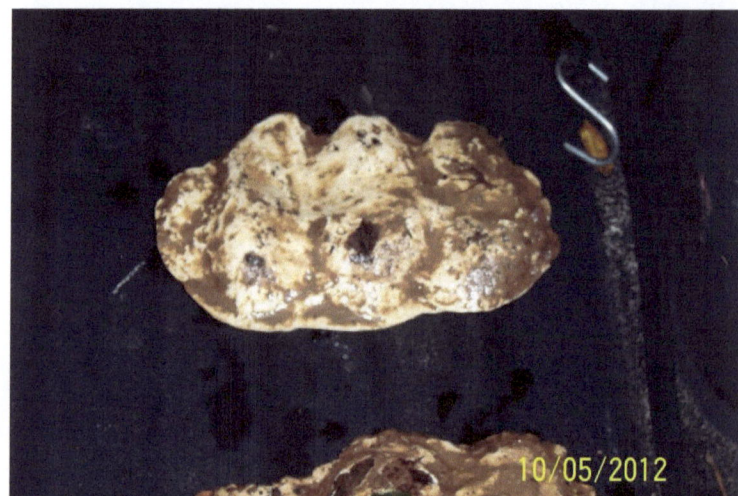

10/05/2012

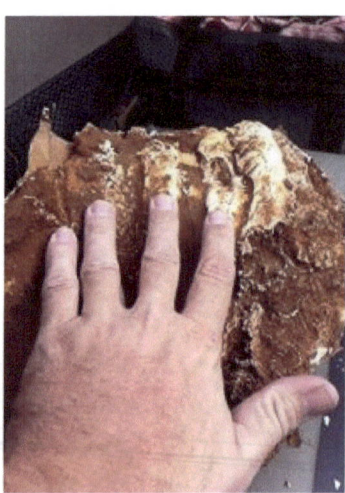

The Oklahoma hand print cast, it dwarfs the researcher's hand here in comparison.

The following pictures are of the knuckle prints found

10/05/2012

Baiting Techniques

In Bigfoot research, many researchers attempt to use bait to attract Bigfoot to their research areas.

While there is no correct way of doing it, there are some things that you should be aware of that may add to your chance encounter of Bigfoot.

The first thing to remember, is that if you put your bait on the ground, whether in "gifting bowls" or directly on the ground, that small animals will eat the food you use as bait. An individual in Oregon claims that no small animals eat out of his "gifting bowls" and only Bigfoot does this.

There is no way a claim like this can hold any water. The woods are full of small animals who will eat whatever they can find, even larger predators will take advantage of an easy meal.

Another individual quite a few years ago, began baiting with a large pile of ears of corn, and began making claims that Bigfoot was coming up and eating the corn. Other wild claims made by the individual required his governing organization to send someone out to verify what he was claiming. What was found, was that deer tracks led up to the pile of corn, and despite the mud around the pile of corn, no Bigfoot tracks were uncovered. When approached with these facts, the individual claimed infringement on his research area, which in actuality was the organization's research area that had been turned over to him.

The truth of the matter, is that if you are going to leave bait on the ground, do not believe that Bigfoot is

the only ones eating it. You have to be ready to admit that smaller animals will be eating what you put out.

This also brings about an ethical question, that by putting out food, you will be feeding the local wildlife, and this could effectively train the wildlife, especially larger predators, to approach humans expecting to be fed. Causing animal attacks on humans is something that should be avoided at all costs.

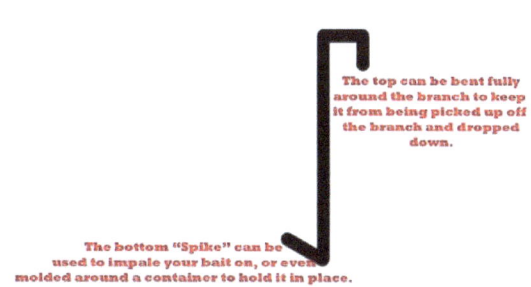

Wrong ways to bait

The MABRC has various ways to do baiting, along with several long-term bait stations. On of those techniques is to hang the bait from a standard wire coat hanger as illustrated in the picture here.

The top can be bent fully around the branch to keep it from being picked up off the branch and dropped down.

The bottom "Spike" can be used to impale your bait on, or even molded around a container to hold it in place.

Hanging your bait this way keeps small animals from pulling up your bait to eat it, and make sure you put it about 6 to 7 feet high, and at least 3 feet from the tree trunk. This will put it at eye level for most Bigfoot. I prefer to impale a bag of butter lover's popcorn on it, and leave it like that.

In the past, MABRC researchers have placed trail cameras on bait hung from tree branches with string or light wire. Raccoons have been watched pulling the bait up to themselves, and removing the bait. By using the sturdy wire of a clothes/coat hanger, it will be nearly impossible for a small animal to pull it up to them. While it can still happen, it's not so easy for them, and if the bait is about 6 foot high in the air, getting to it from the ground is pretty much ruled out too.

While we would show a picture of one actually made, we could not get the picture to show too clear since the wire is small enough that it couldn't show properly.

Another tactic that has been used, is actually credited to Randy "Driveroperator" Harrington for creating it.

While doing a vast majority of his research down in Honobia, Oklahoma, Randy would leave a printed out copy of a picture of Bigfoot standing beside someone with a blue fire dept. shirt on them. Randy would always wear his Fire Dept. sweatshirt while researching there, it was blue. Randy hoped that the Bigfoot would recognize him as being the one

Baiting Techniques (cont.)

leaving the food for them. While initially this was left on the ground, Randy knew that most of the time, small animals would eat it, but in the event a Bigfoot did take it, they would see the picture and hopefully understand.

Several years later, this culminated in the Honobia Walkie-talkie incident, in which it's believed a Bigfoot found a walkie-talkie that had been lost off a researcher's 4 wheeler and held onto it for several days before returning it inside a rock structure left on a trail.

It was attributed to the fact that Randy was wearing his blue sweatshirt at the time, and that the local Bigfoot may have become familiar with him.

Photo A shows Randy's earlier attempts at this technique. Photo B shows D.W. "Darkwing" Lee and Carissa "Splatter" Schulze's attempt to use it in a bait station near Carissa's home. The intent was that since she had lived most of her life in the area, that possibly the Bigfoot would see her picture and maybe begin hanging around her property. Carissa would then be able to spot them coming up. Since the first deployments, Bigfoot-related activity has spiked at Carissa's property. At the bait station itself, it was discovered that nearly 50 juvenile

tracks were found to be going back and forth to the bait area, with even a small tree being removed completely out of the ground when Halloween popcorn balls had been placed in it.

While it could have been a bear ripping the tree up trying to get the bait, the tree was not found laying anywhere close by.

Photo A. Driveroperator's bait and picture.

Photo B. Darkwing and Splatter's bait and picture in use.

While there are multiple other techniques that can be used, the most important fact to remember is that

always make it hard for smaller animals to get to the bait, if you place it at least 6 feet from the ground, and out of reach from adjoining trees or underbrush, when it's taken, you can then say that there is potential for a Bigfoot to be taking it.

Also keep in mind, that in some areas, it is illegal to feed wildlife, so always consult your local wildlife and hunting regulations to insure you are not breaking the law.

If you suspect that a large predator other than Bigfoot is taking your bait, stop immediately from putting out any further food, as this could potentially create an issue where the predator becomes less likely to be afraid of humans and cause an animal attack. It won't be the animal's fault, you aided in training it into thinking all humans will give it food. So please be responsible in the way you do any baiting, you can cause serious injury to yourself, others and even the animals, by being careless in your baiting.

Meals ready to eat

While there are many variants of Meals ready to eat (MREs), the main point is that they can be readily transported without taking up a lot of valuable pack space.

MABRC Researchers use these during expeditions, night hikes, traveling on 4 wheelers into back areas and more. Some versions of MREs have their own heater to heat up the food, usually by adding water or salt water into the package.

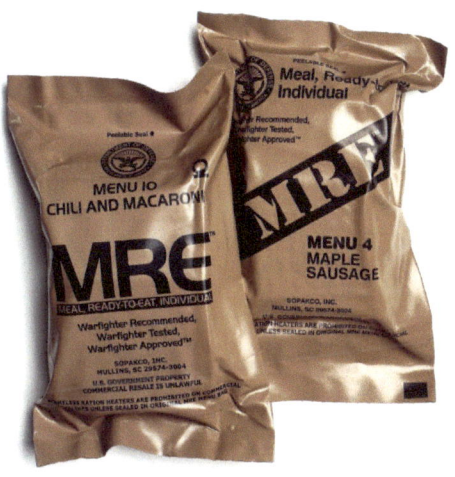

Within 10 minutes, a researcher can have a hot steaming meal to warm their insides with. With an entre, side dish, dessert and other add-ons, this is a complete meal in a vacuum sealed package.

Besides being waterproof, the MREs have a durable shelf life of several years.

Senior Field Researcher Izzy "Goose" Gutierrez is shown chowing down in the field with MREs, if they can keep a growing boy going with enough calories, then it can keep most adult researchers going for days.

You can order MREs online at Amazon.com or get them at most Outdoor stores.

MABRC Press

The **MABRC Press** was put together in order to give the **MABRC** it's own publishing arm. Currently in it's inventory is several Bigfoot Field Guide - In the shadows books, dealing with Audio Analysis and Video Analysis, with Territory Markers Analysis, Starting your own Bigfoot Research, and Casting Tracks coming out in the next few months.

The **MABRC** also has several of the back issues of the Bigfoot Field Guide Magazine available in print.

To order from the **MABRC Press**, visit the **MABRC** Website and click on the link for **MABRC Press**, and you will find the links to buy any of the books and magazines published by **MABRC Press**.

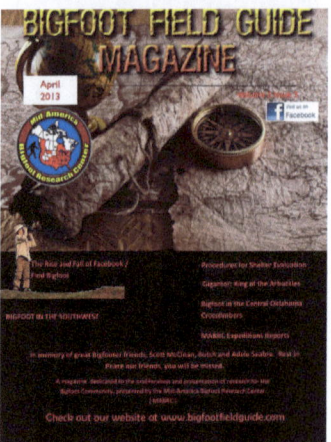

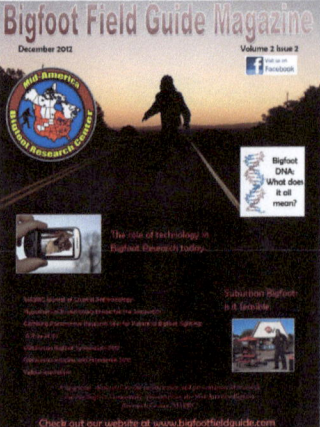

Bigfoot: Past Tense

The Strange Case of Muchalat Harry

Not only children have been the unwilling victims of Bigfoot or Sasquatch as we shall see when reading the tale of the strange case of Muchalat Harry.

The Nuuchahnulth or Nootka Indian tribes were whale hunting Indigenous people of the Pacific Northwest Coast of Canada living on the west coast of Vancouver Island. Muchalat Harry, a seasoned trapper who frequently spent long periods of time alone in the deep woods decided once again to venture into the British Columbian wilderness for several months of trapping. It was the fall of 1928 when Harry packed his supplies and paddled his canoe up to the mouth of the Conuma River and after making his way on foot about 12

miles upstream Harry made camp.

Harry was enjoying his excursion and slept dreaming peacefully at night waking refreshed and eager for whatever the next day would bring. But on one certain night no dream or premonition could have foretold the strange occurrence that befell him. Asleep by the campfire cozily wrapped in blankets, for it was the fall season, he felt his body being jostled, lifted, and shaken. His eyes opened in confusion. As he became aware of what was happening he was gripped by the sudden fear of the

experience. He felt his body being picked up and carried away by a very large creature. Now Harry was strong and tough but try as he may he could not struggle his way free. As he tried to break the hold of the unusually strong arms that held him he saw the creatures face and realized his kidnapper was a very large Sasquatch.

He was not taken very far, probably about 2 or 3 miles and with first light, Harry found himself in what appeared to be a Sasquatch camp and he was the center of attraction. Being surrounded by some 20-odd creatures of all shapes and sizes, male and female alike, they stood starring at him as if to study him.

Harry was scared! This rugged mountain man was terrified! Cautiously Harry moved his eyes glancing around the campsite looking for anything that he might be able to use as protection. All he saw was a large number of bones scattered about the grounds, bones no doubt, left over from who or whatever had been eaten some time before. Harry knew that his bones would soon join them.

Curiously a Sasquatch moved toward Harry and tugged at the woolen underwear that he had worn to sleep the night of the incident. Others also stepped forward and grabbed at this strange thing that surrounded Harry's body still unaware of what it was but they did not harm him they just continued to stare.

At one point during the day the creatures seemed to lose interest in Harry. They disassembled and went about their daily business. Harry searching for a means of escape quickly seized the opportunity and without looking back jumped up and ran as fast as he could barefoot through the woods. He ran for his life, past his campsite,

straight to where his canoe was anchored 12 miles away at the mouth of the Conuma River and headed back to Vancouver Island.

About 3 a.m. on the following morning, Father Anthony, a Catholic missionary living at the time in the Nootka village, heard and was awakened along with other villagers by the screaming and yelling of a voice crying out from the waters near the village. Torches were lit and through the flickering light could be seen a torn and shattered man lying in his canoe. He was barefoot, cold, wet, and exhausted having paddled 45 miles non-stop from the mouth of the Conuma River. His almost lifeless body was carried to a safe warm place in the village and Harry was nursed back to health.

Three weeks had passed before Harry regained his sanity and was well enough to explain what had happened but he refused to tell anyone of his experience. Little bits of information had emerged during that time but not enough to piece together the full story. Feeling close to Father Anthony he later confided in him and revealed the details of what he had gone through. Oh yes, one more thing, over the three week period Harry's hair had turned pure white.

Muchalat Harry never went back to retrieve his belongings at his campsite and Muchalat Harry never went back to the river or into the woods again.

Featured Sighting Report

October 3, 2015

Southeast Adair County, Oklahoma.

Around 9:40 PM.

At the MABRC Base Camp during the 2015 Oklahoma Bigfoot Symposium, a plan was put together for a night hike and listening post. It would include members of the MABRC, BFRO and TBRG at one of the hotspots for Bigfoot activity in Oklahoma.

The plan called for D.W. "Darkwing" Lee to ride a four wheeler up into a valley that was known for Bigfoot activity, traveling about half-way through the 6 mile long area. He would be doing this in hopes of stirring up curiosity of the Bigfoot there and follow him out. Across the creek crossing from the entrance to the valley, the listening post team would take up positions and wait for D.W. to come back out, and drive past them, that way the Bigfoot would not realize there was someone there since D.W. would act like no one was there.

Waiting for the listening post team to go out first, D.W. would give them about 10 minutes to get down the trail.

Since it was a simple run up the valley, something that

D.W. had done many times in the past, he didn't mount the thermal camera on the front of the 4 wheeler as is his method of operation, and he would make the trip alone.

D.W. headed out, passing the hiking listening post team on his way towards the valley, and on into the darkness.

The terrain of the valley is a mix of rocky trails and flat surfaced dirt trails, going through several creek beds. During the first 1/4 mile into the valley, the trail is really rocky, but once D.W. passed this part, he speeded up on the 4 wheeler to get further back into the valley.

Nearly a mile back into the valley, the trail was mainly packed dirt, mixed with some rocks, it also curved several times.

D.W. was near a previous sighting location and a suspected nest structure when he came around a "S" curve.

In his headlights, he observed a sight that surprised him, two large bipedal figures walking down the center of the trail, carrying about an 8

month old calf, weighing approximately 500 pounds across their combined shoulders, walking in-line with each other.

This is the average size of a 500 pound calf, this was the size of calf D.W. saw being carried off.

But what came next was so shocking to D.W., a veteran researcher with 25 different encounters with Bigfoot, that when he returned to the listening post team, he was nearly in shock.

At the second curve of the "S" curve, the back end of D.W.'s 4 wheeler raised up, nearly sending him over the handlebars, the vehicle literally coming to a hard stop.

Looking over his right shoulder behind him, D.W. was able to see the right shoulder and arm of a black Bigfoot.

The next day at the Symposium, the local caretaker of the cattle in the area, informed the MABRC that indeed, an older calf was indeed missing from the herd in the field near the sighting location.

A third Bigfoot had apparently stepped off the side of the trail upon hearing D.W. approaching, and had stepped out behind the 4 wheeler, and grabbed the back bumper of it, stopping it cold, lifting it at least 3 feet off the ground.

Now D.W. could only speculate, but it appeared that the third Bigfoot was trying to prevent him from hitting the other two Bigfoot.

D.W. said it felt like an eternity as the Bigfoot held the 4 wheeler up, but it was perhaps just a second or two, before it released the bumper and dropped the back of it.

In fast order, D.W. gunned the throttle on the 4 wheeler, speeding through the woods to turn around and head back out of the valley.

Once he crossed the creek out of the valley, D.W. found members of the listening post team waiting on him, wondering why he was tearing through the valley.

With steam coming out of the 4 wheeler, D.W. related in between deep breaths what had transpired.

The listening post team made sure that D.W. didn't slip into shock, and escorted him back to camp.

After calming down, Mike "CompresseMike" Hartsell discussed what happened with D.W., and the decision was made for Mike to accompany D.W. back to the location to see if the Bigfoot were still nearby.

D.W. was reluctant, but agreed to go back.

Upon returning to the site of the encounter, a large branch had been placed across the trail.

Actual photo of the tree limb across the trail.

No sign of the Bigfoot still being in the area, it was noted that earlier in the evening, D.W. and Mark "Sawdustt" Newbill had traveled down the same trail and there was no big branches laying across the trail there.

Returning to camp, D.W. felt drained as the adrenalin had stopped flowing, and he turned in to rest.

While D.W. was retiring for the night, other researchers from the MABRC, BFRO and TBRG exam-ined the bumper on the 4 wheeler and discovered that the bumper had been cracked from the force of the Bigfoot stopping it and picking it up.

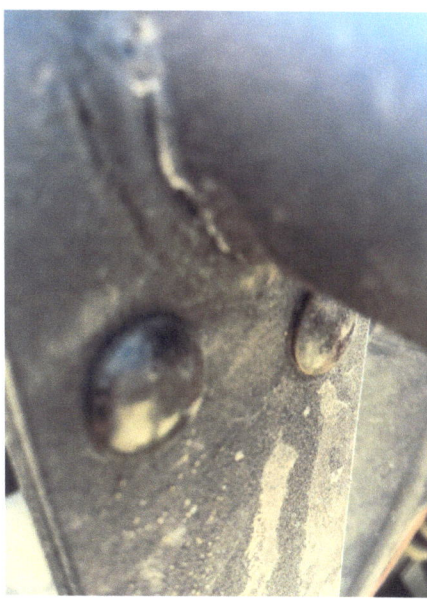

Featured Investigation

Project Bikini Bottom

July 17th-19th, 2015

The original name for this project revealed the location of the project, so it was renamed **Bikini Bottom**, due to the location of Base Camp being near the park swimming area, and the research area being in the bottoms. And yes, we are aware of the Spongebob Squarepants referencing.

Field Team
Squatchfinder
ArkansasTracker
Sawdustt
Goose
Darkwing

Support Team
Sensortech
Biggjimm

Friday Night
The field team had two boats with three thermal cameras, with the first boat crewed by ArkansasTracker and Squatchfinder. The second boat was crewed by Sawdustt, Goose and Darkwing. The boats headed out at 5 pm so that recon could be done on the 3 rivers area where they would be researching later in the dark.

Upon arriving at the entrance to the 3 rivers, the boats stopped in a small cove to get last minute organization done. The first boat had already turned around and would go check out the next cove to see if that was the main channel that was being searched for.

As the second boat proceeded to turn around, a Bigfoot was spotted standing in an opening in the woods in about waist high water.

The second boat turned back around to face the Bigfoot but it had moved off into the flooded woods behind the opening. The first boat was on the other side of the woods in a position that hopefully would have gave them a glimpse of it. Squatchfinder thought he seen the head and shoulders of it with thermal but it was so brief he couldn't obtain a picture of it with the thermal.

The second boat was crewed by Sawdustt, Goose and Darkwing. The boats headed out at 5 pm so that recon could be done on the 3 rivers area where they would be researching later in the dark.

The second boat then joined the first boat and the sighting was discussed.

The boats then set off for the main channel, using depth finders and GPSs to navigate the channel, while occasionally having to move logs and other debris out of the path of the boats. Once through the debris, the boats ended up in the main channel that was fairly clean and deep. Going several miles back along the center river, the boats were finally stopped by a large tree that had fallen across the river, and actually looked like it had been used as a crossing for someone or thing.

It was at this location that Sawdustt deployed his parabolic recorder about 50 feet into the woods, aiming it further inland. It was decided that it would be left in place for 24 hours to record.

After placing the recorder, a glow stick was hung on the tree so that it would be easy to locate in the dark.

The boats then sat in the channel for nearly an hour, as a listening post. Squatchfinder would do some calls, and off in the distance to the east, there were some slightly heard responses.

Boat one then moved downriver about 2000 feet around the bend to set up a second listening post. Squatchfinder did additional calls from that location and the second boat heard a clear response to the east of their position. Unable to get the first boat on the radio to tell them about the vocalization, the second boat moved down to their position to let them know what had happened.

Upon arriving, it was decided to have both boats maintain a listening post together, and this position was held for about an hour before it was discussed to create impromptu bouys to leave along the river to see if the Bigfoot would take them. Glow sticks were inserted into empty gatorade bottles and floated along the river at different intervals. It was well afterdark by this time, and the second boat would then go upriver to where the parabolic recorder was positioned with it's light bar on, in an attempt to get

any Bigfoot curious enough to follow them. Once they arrived at the recorder location, the boat turned around and slowly headed back downstream.

Once they got to where the first boat was sitting at, the second boat passed by it, and the first boat fell in behind with a trolling motor. It was hoped that they might spot any Bigfoot that may be tree peeking at the second boat with it's light bar on.

As the boats went out of the river area to the lake, glow sticks were attached to trees to give a trail back into the area at night.

Finally reaching the lake itself, the boats would separate and go against opposite banks, scanning with the thermals in hopes that maybe a Bigfoot would be at the shoreline and be caught on the thermals. Boat one went along the north shoreline, while Boat two went along the south shoreline.

Both boats finally arrived back at base camp at 1:15 AM, and ArkansasTracker suggested another excursion back into the river areas before daylight. It was agreed to and everyone settled in, getting some rest.

Before 5 AM, ArkansasTracker, Goose and Darkwing set out in Boat one, heading to the river area. Upon arrival it was discovered that the water level had dropped about a foot in the time in between trips.

So since it may not have been possible to recover the parabolic recorder if it dropped any more, the device was recovered.

The other two rivers were also checked out once the sun rose. Several locations were found that would make great listening post spots.

One on the north river would allow the boat to sit below the bank, and by raising the thermal up, it would be able to monitor a 30 to 40 acre field surrounded by woods. This would be the location of the night ops for Saturday night.

Arriving back to base camp, Sawdustt and Squatchfinder were filled in on the details of what had happened during the second trip in.

Goose fell asleep in his chair, so he was moved into the tent on his cot.

ArkansasTracker had to leave, so he loaded up his boat and headed home. After ArkansasTracker left, Darkwing also went to lay down. Sensortech arrived a short while later, and him and Sawdustt went driving around to do some recon on several of the roads near the three rivers area. Squatchfinder went into town to get ice and lunch for everyone.

When Darkwing and Goose woke up, they waited on Sensortech and Sawdustt to return. Sensortech showed Darkwing the lake map he brought and pointed out additional information that really helped bring things on the river into perspective. Squatchfinder arrived back from town, and after everyone ate their lunch, Sensortech headed out to attend a family event that had come up for him.

The game plan for Saturday night was discussed, it was then that the field team realized that the water level had dropped another foot, leaving the remaining boat sitting on land. The remaining team members went down and got the boat back into the water.

Preparing to head out on the boat, the team was aware that Biggjimm had planned to be there during the day sometime. So the team tried several times to contact him to find out where he was at, if he was coming or not. The team had about given up on Jim, and was preparing to leave, with the intention of not returning until the next morning, when Jim called and said he was about 30 minutes away. This changed the daytime game plan, the team would take Biggjimm in for a daylight view of the river area.

As the team set off once again to go into the 3 river area, the boat began taking on water from the high choppy water. At first it was thought that the live well was overfilling, but after beaching several times to bail water and making it to the south river, it was decided to head back since only one boat was left and if it went down, we would have no rescue.

On the way back to base camp, it was discovered that the high choppy water was coming over the gunwale of the boat. With the water like it was, night operations for the second night would be impossible. So once back to camp, the boat was loaded up on the boat trailer and removed from the water. Once on the trailer, Goose removed the drain plug and about 100+ gallons of water poured out.

Sawdustt and Squatchfinder then cooked a great meal of bar-b-que chicken and the team sat around discussing Bigfoot. Squatchfinder would head home about 11:30 pm Saturday night while the rest of the team would crash shortly thereafter. The next morning, the team woke up and began packing up. Lots of lessons learned and return trip is in mind.

Tracks-Distinguishing Features

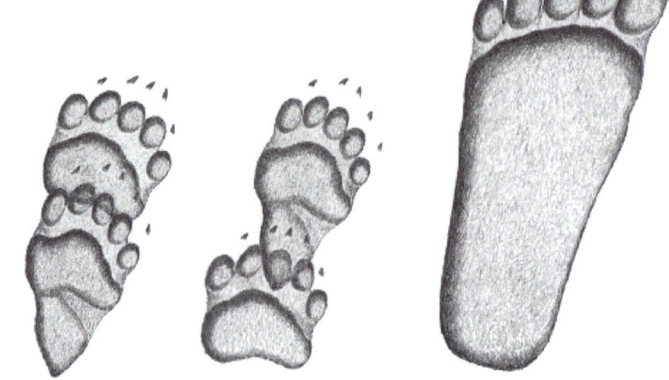

Researchers today appear to find tracks everywhere, even the mature, senior researchers tend to see tracks that are more likely misidentifications.

From bear oversteps, to actual outright hoaxing by individuals, tracks are being brought forward that do not fall into the realm of Bigfoot creating them.

It falls back to the fact that everyone wants so bad to bring in evidence, that they don't hold it to a critical review before throwing it out there to the public as being made by Bigfoot.

One of the biggest claims that makes me bang my head into the wall is when someone posts pictures of a "track" they claim they found, and it's simply a cleared spot on the ground.

In this article, we will show some of the more common misidentifications, some even made by some of the cast on Finding Bigfoot. As I said, the desire of researchers to find evidence is the biggest drawback to finding tracks in the field today.

The more common misidentification is the bear overstep, which in the following graphic, you can see how the bear will overstep the hind foot on top of the front foot track, this will cause an elongated track, that at first glance, will resemble a bi-pedal humanoid track. By studying it closely, the researcher will see the presence of claw marks from the hind foot in the middle of the combined track.

A bear will also not be in-line tracks as shown in the following graphics.

Bear tracks are parallel to each other as shown above.

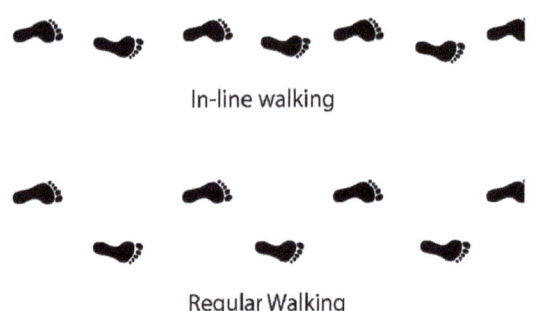

In-line walking

Regular Walking

Human walking (Regular) compared to in-line walking that many believe Bigfoot walks.

With this information, a researcher can discount most tracks that are bear overstep if they just remember these steps to check for.

The next misidentification is that of human feet being responsible for creating the tracks, it's very easy when the toes are clearly visible.

Most Americans have not went barefoot since childhood, but there are still quite a few who will shed their shoes and walk about the woods, grass and even through the mud. A majority of the tracks discovered near water in the mud, is possibly someone discarding their shoes and walking through the mud barefoot to avoid getting their shoes filled with mud.

Researchers who know what they are looking for, can disqualify a track when made by a human by the toes if they are clearly shown.

In the pic below, you will see two feet encased with shoes. Notice the toes, they become scrunched together, in particular, the small toe, it is bent inward from constant wearing of the shoes.

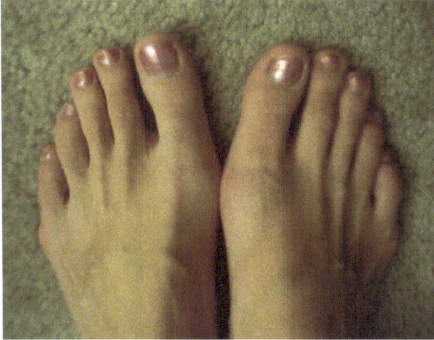

Another picture below shows the inward bent toe.

Compare these with the next photo, which shows the feet of a native in Africa who has never wore shoes

before in their life, compared to that of a European who has worn shoes most of their life. Notice the toes are splayed for the native, while the toes of the European are almost grown together.

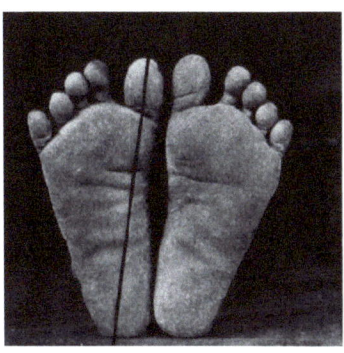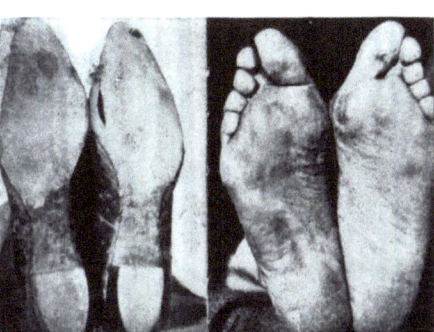

If you come across a track and the toes are smashed together, and the small toe is bent inwards, it more than likely was created by a human, even if it's 13"-15" long, it is within the realm of humans to have feet that long.

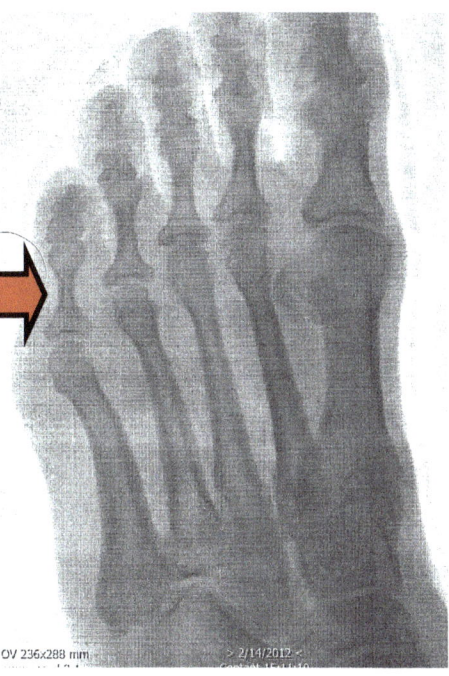

In the above x-ray, you can tell how the bones of the toes have developed for a person who has worn shoes all their lives. The toe bones

are pushed inward, and have grown in that way.

One researcher in Missouri once presented me with pictures of a cast that he had made of a footprint near his home.

One of the features that was standing out, was that the small toe was bent inward. After further investigation, it was discovered the track had been found in a public recreation area, where a lot of the local population of "humans" went to swim, picnic and hang out at. It was obvious that this track came from a human, yet the researcher did not want to accept that, instead, taking the track around with claims that it's a Bigfoot track.

Claims like this, is what sets the Bigfoot Community back on it's heels, the illegitimacy of such a claim makes the public at large remain skeptical.

Another issue that affects track finds, is that of hoaxing. How does a researcher tell if a track has been hoaxed or not.

Most times, it's hard to the average researcher who has not done their homework about the details.

Most hoaxed tracks are created by taking a previous casted track and shoving it into the ground to create an impression for others to find, or even someone cutting out a wood outline of the foot.

When this occurs, you have several signs to look for on a track you find.

The first is called impact ridges and is illustrated by the diagram to the right. Impact ridges are caused by inanimate objects not splaying themselves out properly from the weight of the animal creating it. The bottom of the foot is skin, and because of this, the skin will push out and create what is called "compression lines" as shown in the diagram on the lower right. If someone pushes a cast into the dirt, it can't create compression lines as the cast is an inanimate object, there is no give way like flesh and blood will create.

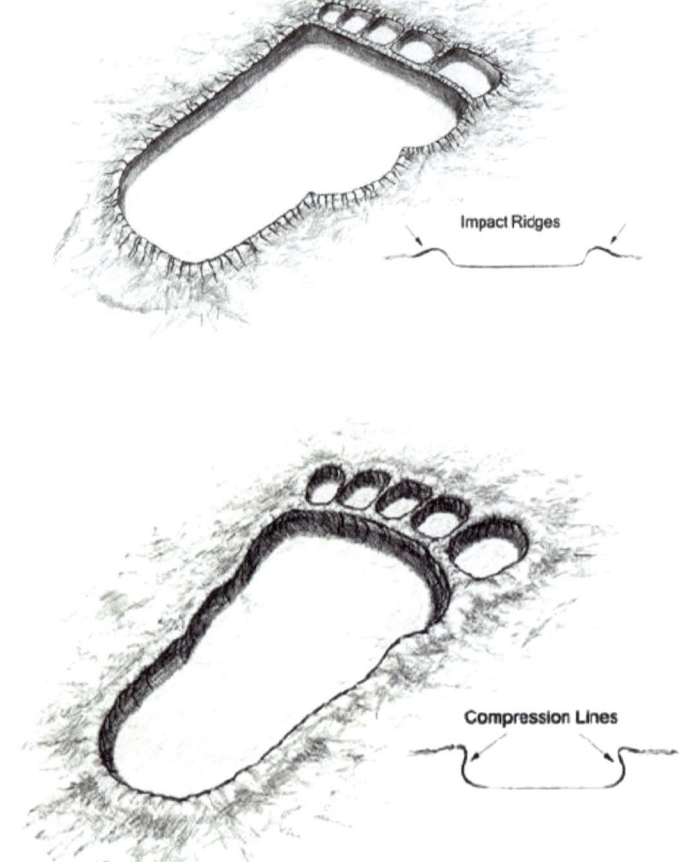

Impact Ridges

Compression Lines

What you end up with, is the impact ridges around the outer edges of the track.

If it was create by a flesh and blood animal, the soul of the foot will push out and create the compression lines from the weight of the animal.

While most hoaxed tracks will occur in sandy, clay or muddy areas, it has been found that hoaxed tracks can be in any terrain. So don't rule out a track as being hoaxed because you found it in rocky terrain or a gravel bar.

Location is another factor, just because it was found 10 miles into the wilderness does not automatically exclude it from being a hoaxed track. Yes, peo-

ple do go back into the wilderness and create hoaxed tracks, even in the likelihood that no one will ever find them.

In the following photos, we will show you how indentions in the ground are usually claimed to be tracks by researchers who have not taken the time to do their homework.

What does that mean? For instance, some researchers will find a trackway of "tracks" in the snow, and immediately claim it's Bigfoot tracks. But when asked if there was packed snow at the bottom of the "purported" tracks, they get defensive.

Why you ask? Because they didn't do their homework. If it was indeed a large 500 to 800 pound bipedal animal walking through the snow, the bottom of the tracks would have compressed snow at the bottom. 95% of the "purported" tracks that are presented are nothing more than smaller animals jumping through the snow, creating the impression that something walked through the area. Foxes in particular will jump up into the air, and landing face first into the snow in search of smaller prey underneath the snow. A fox can literally create a trackway by doing this type of activity.

When there is a viable explanation for what is creating what you view as a track, you should always err on the side of caution and never claim it is a **Bigfoot** track, it will come back to bite you.

Water can create what many researchers will believe are tracks. The photo below is where water evaporated underneath the surface of the ground, leaving a hollow place below the crust, once this collapsed, it formed what several researchers believed was **Bigfoot** tracks.

This is nothing more than a mud puddle that is shaped like a foot, you can see where the water dried over a period of days.

The next picture is a combination of water running off the vegetation and wallowing out a depression in the shape of a foot, this is nothing more than an old dried up mud hole.

Perhaps the most frustrating misidentification for me, is when a gouge in the ground is presented as a **Bigfoot** track. It's almost as if someone will ask me to believe that **Bigfoot's** foot is the equivalent of **Velcro** to the ground, in which ever step they make, rips the sod up and leaves a bare spot there.

Maybe someone used gorilla super glue in order to get **Bigfoot** stuck on the grass? No, this is possibly nothing more than an animal rooting into the grass, it just has the outline of a footprint.

The following pictures show what are commonly misidentified as being **Bigfoot** tracks. Most are indentions on the ground that people allow their minds to shape into **Bigfoot** tracks. Always be skeptical of any tracks or outlines that appear to be tracks, skepticism is your best ally in research.

Paid Expeditions? Are they worth it?

Over the course of the last few years, an influx of groups have formed to provide "Paid" expeditions for anyone willing to pay the money to attend. Some groups have turned it into a fine art, promising encounters on every expedition (S.E. Oklahoma Kiamichi Mountains) to having thermals for you to use while on the expedition.

The **MABRC** does not charge the public to attend their expeditions, and is always willing to share the knowledge of it's researchers. For anyone wanting to attend some of the other expeditions where they have to pay to attend, we recommend that you thoroughly vet the group or individuals that are putting on the expedition. Some individuals have been busted in the past of hoaxing on their expeditions, and this should give anyone pause before handing your money over to someone who guarantees "Bigfoot" activity on their expeditions.

You should also vet (check out the background) the person's experience level according to Bigfoot research. Just because they post a lot on Facebook or have a pretty face, doesn't qualify them to be hosting an event, and making claims of showing you how to conduct Bigfoot research.

Some of the claims

even makes Bigfoot

wonder what they are trying to accomplish.

Outside of making money, most of these paid expeditions do not give you any benefit except to part your money from your wallet or purse.

Truthfully, no paid expedition is worth it to you, as you end up getting a packaged deal, with claims of being in an active area, and promises of Bigfoot activity.

No one can give you an absolute guarantee of Bigfoot activity. Eyeshine, vocalizations and wood knocks can be hoaxed in order to offer you a hook, and once they do that, they reel you in.

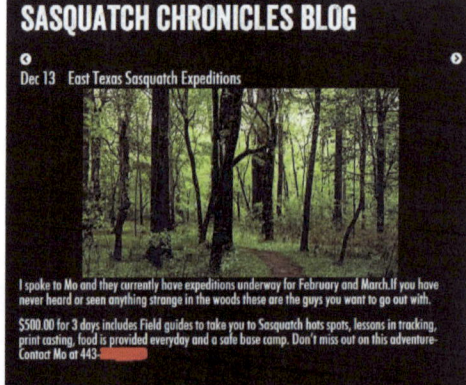

SASQUATCH CHRONICLES BLOG

Dec 13   East Texas Sasquatch Expeditions

I spoke to Mo and they currently have expeditions underway for February and March. If you have never heard or seen anything strange in the woods these are the guys you want to go out with.

$500.00 for 3 days includes Field guides to take you to Sasquatch hots spots, lessons in tracking, print casting, food is provided everyday and a safe base camp. Don't miss out on this adventure-Contact Mo at 443-

★★★ Open Expedition ★★★

3 Guest Speakers!

KENTUCKY BIGFOOT
RESEARCH ORGANIZATION   *"We hunt for evidence, we seek the truth!"*

Western Kentucky   April 7-10, 2016

Bill Brock
Team Rogue
Monsters Underground

Mononga Hela
Cryptologic Linguist
Bigfoot Vocal Expert

Marc DeWerth
Ohio BFRO Investigator

Must be 18 years of age or older. A non-disclosure agreement, a release of liability and a rules/policy form will need to be signed in addition to your $75 non-refundable payment (as space is limited). Guest speakers subject to change.

★Annual   **SOUTHERN SASQUATCH** Expeditions

2016 North Georgia Halloween Expedition
During the Annual Local Fall Festival
October 28 - 29, 2016

Setup Camp or Reserve a Cabin
& Join Us for Night Hiking

$55 per Person to attend both Night Hikes
Limited Space, First Come, First Serve
Contact Angela or Monica to Register

We are taking early Registrations due to the local Fall Festival - Reservations are needed. Upon Registration you will receive information for local campsite and cabin rentals in the area.

Monica Frank Rawlins

Angela Ashton

Ages 21+ Welcome   We are a No Kill Group   Sorry, No Pets Please

The BFRO started this trend years ago, and although I have lots of friends in the group, I do have to hold the **BFRO** responsible for this upsetting trend that is now occurring in the **Bigfoot Community.**

They have transformed it into a business model, that now others attempt to imitate.

The usual result for people going on the expeditions with the **BFRO,** is that they end up offering those more promising individuals a role with the group.

While this may be beneficial, you still end up having to pay a fee, and hope that a roll of the dice lands you a position with the group.

If you want to part ways with your money, then by all means, pay to attend one of these expeditions. The standard promises seem to be night hikes, listening posts, sitting around a camp fire and getting to be around so-called "Well-known" celebrity researchers.

Do your research with due diligence for any group or individual that offers their expeditions for a fee.

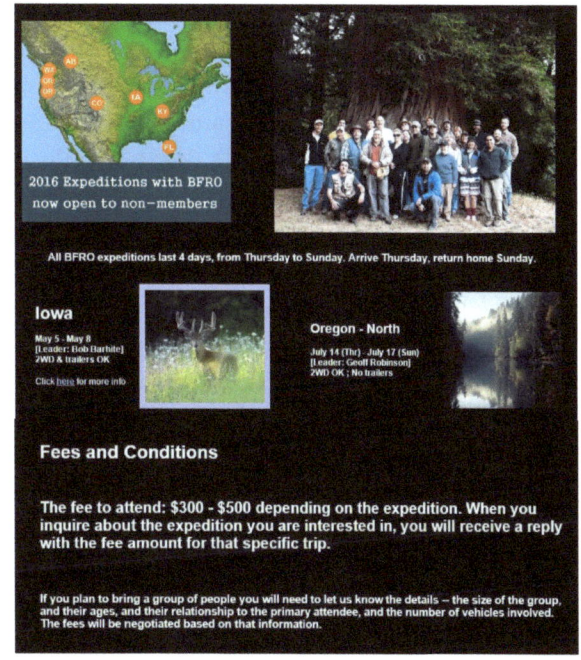

If you find a group or individuals that are willing to take you for free on their expeditions, you may find yourself being asked to sign a **NDA (Non-disclosure Agreement)** to safeguard the location, and asked to follow their rules or protocols, but if they are truly willing to give you the benefit of their experiences and knowledge, you should take that opportunity, but we recommend you still do your due diligence on

finding out more about them before going out with them.

How many years have they been active in research?

What type of evidence have they brought in, in recent years?

What is their belief system as far as Bigfoot goes?

Are they into the "Woo" side of Bigfooting, or into the "Flesh and Blood" side.

Are they no-kill or pro-kill? Do they actively carry firearms?

Do they allow alcohol or drugs on their expeditions?

All these questions and more should always be asked of either "paid" or "free" expeditions.

Save your money instead to buy research equipment that will aid you in doing your own Bigfoot research.

Audio Analysis In Bigfoot Research

Order your copy of the Bigfoot Field Guide—In the Shadows: Audio Analysis in Bigfoot Research now, learn how the MABRC Researchers use the software, equipment and tactics to obtain their audio and results from the field. Available now at Createspace.com at https://www.createspace.com/5675002 or from Amazon at http://www.amazon.com/Bigfoot-Field-Guide-Analysis-Research-ebook/dp/B013U6TDYY

Get your copy today, and learn how the researchers conduct audio analysis.

Paranormal Incident Reports-Bigfoot?

Starting several years ago, **MABRC Senior Field Researcher Jim "Biggjimm" Whitehead** began a project where he went through various paranormal/ghost sites online to see if they had any reports that could have been misinterpreted as being Bigfoot related instead of being a ghost.

What Jim discovered was a vast majority of sightings were indeed misidentifications, as reports spoke of hairy ghosts walking through the woods or graveyards.

It was a massive undertaking, in which Jim first started with Oklahoma, his home state, and poured through the reports one site at a time, one report at a time.

What he came up with was an interesting number of sightings that were added to the **MABRC** sighting data.

The map below reflects that data along with the numbers for sightings actually submitted to online sighting reports for Bigfoot.

As you can see, the numbers increase dramatically across the state when compared to the data of reports submitted to Bigfoot researchers. (See opposite page)

The numbers were pretty impressive, leading Jim to give a presentation at the 2015 Oklahoma Bigfoot Symposium over how he obtained the data, and the interesting facts that he discovered. To see the presentation, you can find the link at the **MABRC Website** on the Bigfoot Field Guide tab.

www.mid-americabigfoot.com

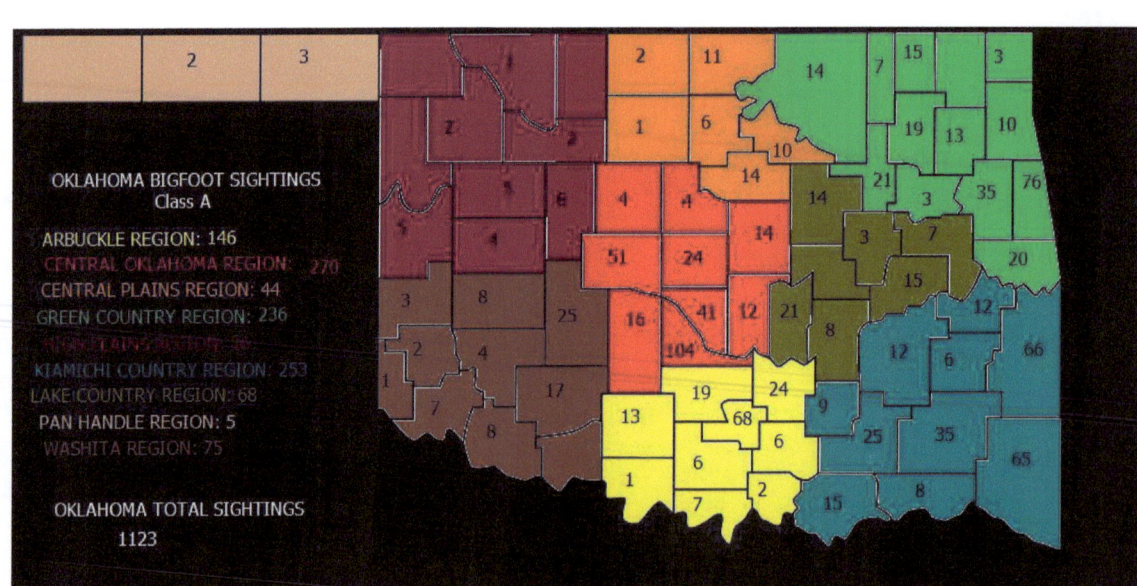

OKLAHOMA BIGFOOT SIGHTINGS
Class A

ARBUCKLE REGION: 146
CENTRAL OKLAHOMA REGION: 270
CENTRAL PLAINS REGION: 44
GREEN COUNTRY REGION: 236
HIGH PLAINS REGION:
KIAMICHI COUNTRY REGION: 253
LAKE COUNTRY REGION: 68
PAN HANDLE REGION: 5
WASHITA REGION: 75

OKLAHOMA TOTAL SIGHTINGS
1123

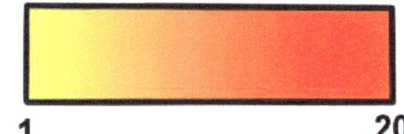

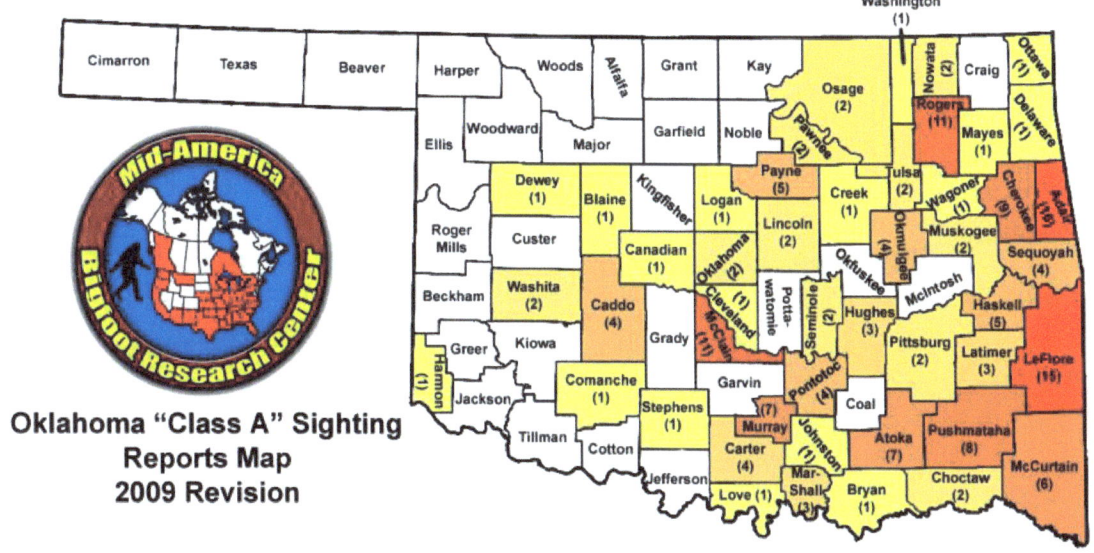

Oklahoma "Class A" Sighting
Reports Map
2009 Revision

www.mid-americabigfoot.com

Joining the MABRC as a member

What does it take to join the Mid-America Bigfoot Research Center as a member? Unlike other groups, we have no membership fees, everyone contributes what they can, when they can, and they subsidize their own research.

From expeditions to conferences, the MABRC has a host of activities going on for it's members, and members are also the first to see evidence submitted to the MABRC before it's released to the public.

To join as a member, go to the MABRC website and fill out the membership application, and once submitted, the MABRC Membership Coordinator will conduct a phone interview with you and you hopefully will be on your way to becoming a full-fledged MABRC Researcher or Analyst.

Even if you consider yourself an armchair researcher, the MABRC led the way with designating armchair researchers as Analysts and putting them to work behind the scenes so join now.

WWW.MID-AMERICABIGFOOT.COM

What is evidence?

At the 2015 Arkansas Bigfoot Conference, D.W. "Darkwing" Lee gave a presentation about evidence that many found enlightening. It discussed "What is evidence?" in Bigfoot Research, and in this article, we will revisit his presentation.

Definition of Evidence

..the available body of facts or information indicating whether a belief or proposition is true or valid.

Evidence in Bigfoot Research

.. the available body of facts or information indicating that Bigfoot exists to satisfy science's protocols.

A monumental task!!

Evaluating evidence

•He receives huge amounts of evidence to analyze weekly.

•MABRC Members know he is skeptical of all evidence, most skeptical of his own evidence.

•Not an expert, but he use a lot of common sense and skepticism when doing analyzing evidence.

• He always use "Possible" or "Purported" when presenting evidence.

Some evidence he receives for review

The above photo is what is usually sent to D.W. for his review and input. This was one that D.W. pulled off the Internet at random to prove a point. When he is told there are numerous Bigfoot in the photo, and he doesn't see them, he will send it back for clarification to what is there. He usually is sent back the photo with red circles showing where the Bigfoot are supposedly at.

D.W. found himself in disbelief when several audience members approached him after the presentation, saying they could see the Bigfoot in it. This was simply a stock photo used to illustrate his point.

But as D.W. would state in his presentation, "I am presented with evidence that people have hopes is Bigfoot, yet after I analyze it, it turns out to be misidentification or the high hopes of the person that something is Bigfoot."

Evidence Categories

•Physical evidence

•Audio evidence

•Photographic evidence

•Video evidence

•Thermal evidence

Physical Evidence

•Tracks/Handprints (Casts)

•Structures/Markers

•Hair samples

•Blood samples

•Other body fluid samples

•DNA

Body fluids Evidence

•Feces

•Urine

•Mucus

•Other fluids not mentionable.

DNA

•Ketchum DNA study is not credible.

•Sykes DNA study is still up for debate.

•Most DNA samples submitted have been collected unprofessionally and has been contaminated.

•Proper procedures and protocols must be followed to avoid contamination.

Audio Evidence

•Recordings

•Vocalizations

•Witness narration.

•Recordings are analyzed.

Photographic Evidence

•Digital photos

•Film photos

•Photos found on the Internet

Received last night

D.W. then discusses about a photo sent to him the night before the conference, purportedly showing a Bigfoot walking behind a tree.

Further examination revealed it to be a person wearing blue jeans and boots, and upon telling the person who took it what the analysis revealed, he was told he didn't know what he was doing. But here is the analyzed photo to show what D.W. seen.

Video Evidence

• Backs up the witness' account.

• Allows reviewing and analyzing to either rule out or confirm something was there.

• YouTube has become a curse for the Bigfoot Community.

Thermal Evidence

• Video

• Photographs

• Gives us insight into the darkness previously only Bigfoot's domain.

• Allows us to observe habits of Bigfoot without disrupting their activities.

• Gives us the ability to see in the dark.

• Is it proof positive?? No.

What do we do with the evidence?

Each piece of evidence is like a piece of a puzzle. By itself, a single piece shows only a small part of the picture, but once multiple pieces are put together, the picture starts to become clearer and filled out.

Interpreting the evidence/data

Taking the evidence, we put it side by side with other evidence and begin to paint a picture of where activity occurs, and where it's likely to occur again. The aerial shot shown above has locations marked of activity above a roadside trash dump, and provides the researchers with an idea of which direction the local Bigfoot approach and leave the dumpsters.

Correlating the data

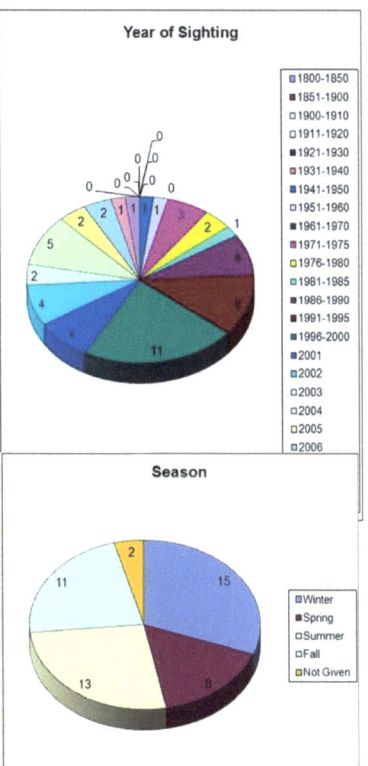

The above charts shows data retrieved from all Class "A" sightings in Oklahoma, it shows the most sightings occurred between 1996-2000 and the most common season that encounters occur is winter. This gives researchers an idea of when the best times are to have an encounter with Bigfoot.

All told, evidence is important to Bigfoot research as long as it's reviewed properly.

An old hoax resurfaces..

Tomagami Island Photos

Time and time again, these photos appear on Facebook, with someone to lazy to do any real research on the photos before asking others, what do you know about these? And as usual, those who know nothing about the history of the Bigfoot Community will speak up and proclaim it to be the best photos out there.

Back in 2007, a MABRC Researcher Rob "ElectricBigfoot" Gaudet was approached by the person behind these photos. From the get-go, alarm bells began going off, as Rob was requested to keep this all quiet and that specialists and experts have looked at the photos and proclaimed it authentic.

A week later, the photos began appearing in the open at the Bigfoot Forums, and the person who had contacted Rob was deliberately putting them out there.

The ruse soon became apparent that the original contact with Rob was in hopes that he would go ahead and post the photos despite the promise him and the MABRC had made to stay quiet on this matter.

The "Bigfoot" in the photo had been identified by MABRC Researchers the second day of having received the photos. It was a costume that could be bought from Halloween online stores. It had been modified with extra hair around the face,

but it was the same mask.

Additional photos began appearing, including so-called "comparison" photos, in which an individual was photographed standing on the opposite side of the fallen tree from the "Bigfoot". The problem was though, that the person standing in the photo was well over 20 feet farther away, giving the impression that the "Bigfoot" was over 7 feet tall. This was noticed immediately by MABRC researchers.

As the story continued to fall apart, it was soon discovered that a movie was being made

was posted by accident on YouTube.

While it was quickly re-

Tomagami
Bigfoot 2007
GM

concerning the adventures of a gentleman, who was lost in the woods. It all came to a head though when it was discovered that a pre-release version of their movie trailer

moved, the MABRC had already downloaded the video as evidence that this was nothing more than an attempt to garner attention for the movie being made.

The movie's title was "The Man God Forgot" and the trailer showed the same suit and mask raising up, then walking off to the left of the screen. It was deemed a hoax on a massive scale, yet on occasion, someone too lazy to do their own research on the photo before posting it, will get it making the rounds again on Facebook.

To the left photos, show a close up of the original close up sent to the MABRC, followed by the comments of MABRC Researcher Rob Gaudet surrounding the events of the photo's transfer to him and the conditions set forth.

The first photo to the top right is the full photo sent, you will notice the name on it, the man involved was named Jim Jardineau, but misspelled his own name.

The middle right photo supposedly shows the comparison photo of the man returning to pick up his tools. Notice that he is standing to the rear of the rootball, approximately 20 feet or more behind where the supposed "Bigfoot" was standing.

The bottom right photo was the comparison photo showing the size difference between the man and the "Bigfoot", again, the difference in position clearly makes it appear that the "Bigfoot" is 8'6" tall, this is a deliberate attempt to hoax in the MABRC's opinion.

When the photo begins making rounds again, no one appears to notice that the angle is what causes the size difference, instead, many just assume that the comparison is correct.

Tomagami Islands Bigfoot
Jmi Jardineau (GEM)2007

Jim's return 3 days later to get the gear.
copyright
Helmedia / 2008

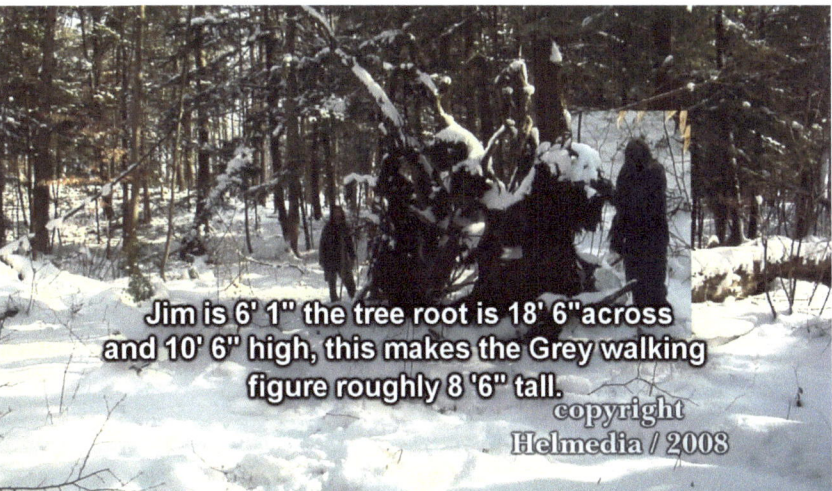

Jim is 6' 1" the tree root is 18' 6"across and 10' 6" high, this makes the Grey walking figure roughly 8 '6" tall.
copyright
Helmedia / 2008

The screen capture to the top right is the suit as it appears to be standing up in the trailer for "The Man God Forgot". Once it was announced by the Bigfoot Community that it had been found, the producers of the movie did everything they could to get it removed from the Internet. Currently, anytime the trailer gets posted by a Bigfoot Researcher, it gets served with Copyright infringement and taken down.

Why does this continue to be taken down, possibly because the producers thought they could generate a lot of buzz in the Bigfoot Community with their fake "Bigfoot" costume, and maybe get the mainstream media involved to give it publicity. Once it backfired, they wanted to remove the evidence.

The bottom right two photos are of the mask used to create the "Bigfoot" in the trailer and photos.

If you zoom in on the "Bigfoot" in the photos, you will see that it does indeed match the mask shown here, with a few extra strands of hair attached.

So anytime you see photos of this online, it continues to surface about every six months. A second attempt at producing photos of a "Bigfoot" on the Tomagami Islands was released a few years ago of a "Bigfoot" walking atop a pile of logs. Due to the past hoax, it too was deemed to be a hoax, as it's method of operation of being produced matched the previous hoax almost to a "T".

IN MEMORIAM

Julius E."Smokey" Crabtree

For a great number of older researchers, the movie "The Legend of Boggy Creek" is perhaps the single most polarizing event that inspired many of us into Bigfoot Research.

At the heart of that movie was Smokey Crabtree, a real life resident of Fouke, Arkansas. It was with great sadness when we all learned that at the age of 88, Smokey passed away on January 16, 2016 in Fouke, Arkansas.

His official obituary reads: "[Julius E. Crabtree] was a Nazarene, a retired welder, contractor, publisher, and had owned the Big Stop Grocery Store in Fouke. He served our country as a Merchant Marine, was a member of the Masonic Lodge, VFW, and Pipeliners Union 798. He had also been a boxer and Golden Gloves Champion. He was preceded in death by two sons, Tommy Crabtree and Lynn Crabtree, and a grandson, Jeremy Knight. Survivors include his wife, Fran Crabtree of Fouke, Arkansas, two sons and daughters-in-law, Travis and Mary Crabtree of Mt. Dora, Florida, and Jay and Toni Crabtree of Texarkana, Arkansas,

one daughter and son-in-law, Debbie and John Knight of Sparkman, Arkansas, ten grandchildren, and a number of great-grandchildren."

With the death of Charles B. Pierce, the director of the movie, "The Legend of Boggy Creek" we can only pray that Charles and Smokey are up there kicked back together enjoying a beer and discussing how they should do another movie together.

God Bless you Smokey, you have made your place in the history of Bigfooting.